THE HAUNT

THE HAUNT

LIZ GREEN

wtaw press

SANTA ROSA, CA

Copyright © 2025 Elizabeth Green

All rights reserved. No part of this publication may be reproduced or transmitted in any form or by any means without written permission from the publisher, except in the case of brief excerpts or quotes embedded in reviews, critical essays, or promotional materials where full credit is given.

This book is a memoir. It reflects the author's present recollections of experience over a period of time. Some names have been changed, some events have been compressed, and some dialogue has been re-created.

Edited by Peg Alford Pursell
Cover photo detail: Inga Seliverstova
Author portrait © Giuliano Lupinetti

Library of Congress Cataloging-in-Publication data is on file with the Library of Congress.

ISBN: 979-8-9877197-1-8 (paperback)
ISBN: 979-8-9877197-2-5 (ebook)

WTAW Press
PO Box 2825
Santa Rosa, CA 95405
www.wtawpress.org

WTAW Press is a not-for-profit literary press. This publication is made possible by the generous contributions from individual donors, public arts organizations, and private foundations.

In memory of

Olinda Buffone Catanzaro, "Biggie"

The Haunt

Man can only escape from the laws of this world in lightning flashes. Instants when everything stands still, instants of contemplation, of pure intuition, of mental void...

–Simone Weil

I didn't grow up in a mansion—the one my mom and stepdad, software engineers, could eventually afford in western New Jersey. At twenty-four, I'd escaped living with them when I'd moved for college. Their house was generic, cavernous, a McMansion that had been built with a crop of others in 1990. On either side of its affluent, isolated street, Rick Road, swaths of fields and woods spread as far as I could imagine.

Decades before, our first hometown had been Fords, New Jersey, 1.89 square miles, not far from Staten Island and minutes from the Atlantic Ocean. Not the fun, idyllic ocean, an alluring destination, but an ocean comprised of garbage and medical waste. Few people have heard of Fords, a non-place. I've had to say I'm from "near New Brunswick," a gritty, vibrant little city home to Rutgers University, which is neither close nor remotely similar to Fords.

Once your family moved away from Fords and your world grew larger, even though Fords hosted your earliest, formative memories, you abandoned all connections to it. You had no roots.

Near the end of my brief marriage, I rode in the back seat of my stepdad's Lexus on the way home to the McMansion from The Perryville Inn, the restaurant where we'd had a family dinner. Pitch-dark county road. Clusters of trees floating past. As I looked out the flickering screen of the window at the twisting, bare boughs, many intertwined, something *happened*. A hit of some knowledge. A truth, though I can't say now about what.

My stepdad had been a reliable part of my life since I was five. Hints of something off with him showed up when I was in my early thirties. Aberrations in his behavior. My brother and I conferred over the phone privately.

We didn't tell my mom. She'd acquired twenty cats who all lived in the bedroom she shared with my stepdad. Most were babies, like Tweeter, a cross-eyed ragdoll kitten she'd found in a field.

My mom had always brought animals into our lives; they were her soft spot. She couldn't set eyes on a cat or puppy, in a store at the mall or on the side of the road, without an urgent impulse to save it. But now her collection of animals amped up. It was as if soon she'd experience an overwhelming need for another. The master bedroom had accumulated a plethora of scratching posts and cat trees and toys that squeaked or tinkled.

For his part, my stepfather took to walking around their house with a handgun tucked in his workout shorts.

Throughout their marriage, he'd pursued different interests—or "fads," my mom called them. He excelled at each pursuit, before he would move on and plunge full throttle into another new passion.

Over the years, he'd gotten deep into meditation and followed a guru who lived in India, competed in volleyball at a nude beach, banged out "Rhapsody in Blue" over and over on our piano, sold NuSkin cosmetic and hair products, studied Aikido, saved lives serving on the local Rescue Squad, knelt at Catholic masses, and spelunked in leviathan-like caves all over the country and in Mexico. Then guns. Anything worth doing is worth overdoing, was his motto.

People who have difficulty with people, and I include myself, seem to have special relationships with animals in which they can finally lower their guard. Maybe an innocent parrot is the only being you can feel completely safe with.

After my marriage failed, at thirty, I moved from Alabama, where I'd lived with my husband. My stepdad flew south—because my mom made him—and drove my Penske truck from Auburn to the small supportive community of Ithaca. The yellow rectangle sped ahead of my car like a kind of beacon for a thousand miles.

In the mid-1990s, I'd gone to college nearby to Ithaca in a rural, economically depressed region that locals call Central New York or the Southern Tier. After graduating, I'd settled in Ithaca for a few years, working minimum-wage jobs at Stella's Café and The Bookery before moving away for grad school.

THE HAUNT

Downtown, with its rectangular brick storefronts, is one of those nostalgic remnants of the 1800s at the center of many small towns across the country. North Aurora Street had a florist, a glimmering row of restaurants, and Collegetown Bagels, also known for pastries and soup. In Ithaca, you gravitated to North Aurora or to the Commons, a pedestrian area surrounded by cafés, the bookstore Autumn Leaves, a head shop, etcetera, and with little pagodas in the center where dreadlocked white guys played Hacky Sack. An apple harvest festival took place there in the fall, and ice sculptures whimsically sprung up every winter, including one that resembled a fanciful throne you could sit on. People loved to have their pictures taken in the frozen seat.

A cult—everyone knew it was—ran one of the coffee shops. The workers never got haircuts. The shop had the best, freshest sandwiches and yerba mate, so it was popular. The male workers, especially, were always after you to convert to whatever had solved their lives, while they shaped fleeting patterns in foam on your latté.

I started spending a lot of time zoning out at Just A Taste, a restaurant that offered low-key, eclectic fine dining. There I met Nicky.

My mom and I sat by the window at Just A Taste, with a highly coveted view of downtown. Nicky waited on us, exuding flirtatiousness, caring vibes. He was rangy, tall, with muscly, beautifully tan arms, a wide, expressive mouth, and eyes that tilted up at the corners like an elf's. We both thought he was hot. When he and I would begin dating several months later, I'd learn he always wore vintage button-down shirts like the ones he sported at work. Their colors and patterns seemed touchably soft, like him.

It's like I'm running a hundred-mile

marathon, and I get to the ninetieth mile and I just can't finish it, my stepdad would tell my mom when he left her, drawing from his true experience of the Vermont 100: 170,000 feet, thirty hours.

When I was in kindergarten, my stepdad and mom wed in the judge's chambers at the courthouse. The paperwork for both of their divorces had been finalized that same week.

After, I saw my dad every few months. "Bio-Dad"—as he and I joked—is a highly solitary person who designed missile defense systems and who has remained single.

For us four kids—two from my stepdad's first marriage, my half-brother, and me—my stepfather did all the mundane stuff a dad does. He balanced on a scary-tall ladder to sling lights around our holly tree and tackled whatever other chore my mom assigned him. She had a genius for interior design, the antique and the ornamental, and she held intense opinions about how everything should be done. Each season, he drove us all around in his Taurus station wagon, sedately, so my mom could see the holiday luminaries.

By the time I was in high school, we had moved from Fords to Middlesex, another small town that no non-local had heard of. People my age always pointed out the "sex" in its name. Still, Middlesex was nicer than Fords—tranquil, with more space between houses, most of them graceful Victorians.

I learned about architectural styles from my mom first, and I'd later learn more from Nicky in Ithaca. My mom and I traveled to fancy neighborhoods to admire unique or elaborate buildings that inspired her. She thrilled at the sight of a mansard roof or a Tudor.

Despite living in the same houses for years, my stepdad and I were wildly dissimilar. Our interactions with each other had three settings: polite, indifferent, or hostile.

THE HAUNT

I was the only kid who wasn't his biological child. I was outside my own family, in a sense.

He'd moved in with my mom and I, in Fords, at the end of my parents' volatile, seven-year marriage. This new, young guy my mom loved was thin, very tall, handsome, and poor. All he had was a parrot named Mr. Bill and the clothes he wore. Clothing his ex-wife had sewn for him.

Mr. Bill was gratingly loud and required a lot of attention. My stepdad began draping Mr. Bill's cage with a cloth, 24/7, to muffle the lonely, aware squawks coming from within. Eventually, my parents rehomed him with a parrot-loving family.

This new, fake dad complained about the nursery rhymes I listened to quietly on a little-kid record player before sleep. He felt I shouldn't need such extra pampering. As if going to bed without listening to music was more self-reliant. He also said my mom shouldn't help me button my shirts.

He wanted the same for all the kids: we

should be capable and independent, set up for success. Unfortunately, I lacked initiative, lived in my imagination, and huddled on the bathroom floor during thunderstorms—the only safe place according to my mom, who always pointed out worst case scenarios.

I felt most connected to my stepdad when we weren't speaking. When he blasted Prince or Dire Straits on the stereo in our living room or in the car on long drives, I could drift away on pulsing bass and ecstatic guitar riffs.

The luminaries in Middlesex were white paper lanterns, ephemerally displayed. Every year, it was tradition for everyone on our street and on the surrounding ones, named for trees—Hazelwood, Beechwood—to make them from paper bags, candles, and some cat litter to anchor the candles. On Christmas Eve, our suburb felt otherworldly, with the lanterns' fairytale mood lighting and sometimes falling snow. If anyone failed to set the luminaries out or placed them improperly—the glowing little bags, insides fluttering, lining driveways and sidewalks in uniform rows—the effect would've been ruined.

In Ithaca, Nicky and I developed rituals, giving me a sense of permanence. "Margs," he called them, every Monday at Viva Taqueria. Late-night cocktails at Felicia's Atomic Lounge, where I sipped chocolate martinis and he drank the 57 Chevy made with Chambord and muddled raspberries.

He talked about his house.

Nicky owned an aging, rundown green Victorian in a part of downtown the cops constantly patrolled. Emergency lights reflected on branches, flashed into the clouds, and pulsated on the sides of faded houses. When he wasn't waiting tables at Just A Taste, he worked on restoring the Victorian, meticulously sanding away layers of paint, stripping everything down to the original wood. Unveiling the past.

At Felicia's, I once secretly timed him talking about the house. Forty minutes before I could say anything.

I'd settled into a garden-level apartment in Fall Haven, a brick complex next to the 150-foot waterfall, Ithaca Falls. Placed high in the living room walls, the windows were wide in the mid-century modern style of post-World War II. They faced a hillside, by turns an impossible green that glowed on my walls or a snowy brightness harsh on my eyes. Most of my neighbors were elderly and eventually left for nursing homes or died. When I got tipsy, which was often, lying on the wall-to-wall carpeting, I cried over a stack of photos that documented my relationship with my husband, from start to end.

Five years had passed since the first-ever shot taken of my husband and I squinting outside at a crafts market in Mesilla, New Mexico. His arm curled around my shoulder.

The last photo in the stack was of our fluffy orangey cat now gone blind. I wept over this image of my cat settled contentedly on a nest of torn shiny wrapping paper scattered on the bed my husband and I had shared.

I'm left with how I've always been seeking. The family part of my life a zone of constant movement. You could call it chaos, uncertainty; psyches and commitments in transition or transit; flux. Disappointment of expectations, dashed hopes, hard truths.

I find an oasis—restaurant or bar—where I can sit with a book or friend or lover or, most often, by myself and feel held in that space by all the staff's efforts to make the encounter special. The shade of lighting, style of chairs and tables, color of the walls and their displays of objects and images, the menus presenting possibilities of tastes, aromas, textures: all curating an experience. A reality.

For years after I'd moved out, my husband, who taught creative writing, was stuck in our house in Auburn, applying for academic jobs elsewhere. Raised in the Pacific Northwest, he'd always felt deeply isolated in the South.

I closed the door to your office–to save on the electricity bill, he said on the phone just after I'd left him.

In Ithaca, I worked for a Tibetan Buddhist press. I swam in waterfall pools and shared joints at bonfires when they were offered to me. I walked everywhere, even in bitter-cold conditions. Often, and unpredictably, I was so depressed the muscles in my face barely moved.

Sometimes when I try to visualize

a loving, spiritual presence, a representation of God, I see my grandmother's face. Her soft Italian eyes, almost unbearably kind. It always surprised me that they were brown like mine, because her hair was an improbable red. During my childhood, she wore it in a bun, and even though the color was fading, the shimmering ginger hue suggested how brilliant it had been.

In 1994, home from college on a break, I sat on her hospital bed at JFK University Medical Center after her second heart bypass surgery, sobbing about my love life, unable to concentrate on anything else—like the fact that I should behave differently, in a way that won't stress her heart.

Her eyes said she was with me in my feelings and sad that I'm suffering, beaming total acceptance and support. She couldn't verbalize these sentiments because of her aphasia from multiple strokes. But at the same time, she existed in a place removed from my sadness. And she didn't understand it, my suffering, so small compared to everything she'd been through in her long life.

The previous year, she'd lost her beloved of over forty years. Lung cancer. I'd fallen apart throughout my Pop Pop's funeral services. A fiery, Sicilian American patriarch, his hair jet-black into his eighties, he'd always shown his softest side to me and was more a father than grandfather. When very young, I'd stayed at my grandparents' often and was confused about who my parents were.

My grandmother, called Biggie for Big Mom, had always moved easily through the world, unlike me. Under five feet tall, with vivid, delicate, bird-like expressions, she wasn't big—but I'd made up the name for her as a small child. I'd needed something that felt cozier than "grandmother" for her. The nickname caught on and everyone, even random adults she'd just met, called her Biggie.

No matter what inner intensity she experienced, that lady was serene. Never in a bad mood. She'd quickly make personal connections that often became lifelong. With the butcher at A&P, who became her good friend. With the family of two doctors from India and their children, who moved in across the street: the equally affectionate, uplifting Ayyagaris became a close part of our family—growing up, I was often at their or their relatives' houses.

To everyone my grandmother knew, she'd mail tender-hearted greeting cards, postcards of pie recipes, or souvenirs from countries she and Pop Pop traveled to after his retirement, Franklin Mint ornaments. In her presence, I felt safe and important. An effusive, warm optimism was part of how she took care of people.

After her strokes, she'd say things she didn't intend and rocked an edgy sense of humor. Once, trying to politely describe my youngest brother's behavior, she called him a little bastard. Years later, when I'd phone from Ithaca and ask how she was, she might respond, *I'm twenty-one and gorgeous.* Or:

Reading the Bible. She'd laugh, a dark, subversive belly laugh. She was paralyzed on one side of her body.

In her hospital room at JFK, she looked at me like I was the only person in the world, the most special being she'd ever seen.

Today, I can't accurately envision Biggie's eyes anymore: trying to is like watching an eclipse through a pinhole.

Around Easter of 2006, I was visiting the McMansion, a three-hour drive from Ithaca. The time I'd later think of as *before.*

Late one night, I slipped down the carpeted stairs to get a snack from the kitchen but stopped short when I saw my stepdad sitting at the dining room table. He was alone with his laptop open and glowing, completely unaware of my presence. The song "You're Beautiful" by James Blunt played.

Instantly, it was clear: I was eavesdropping on something private and weirdly painful to me. He had a certain look. Enraptured. It was in the way he was listening in the bluish pool of light from his screen. Like he was reminiscing about some thrilling, beloved, new person. Some stranger.

I still can't bear to listen to "You're Beautiful"—shallow, whiny—if I ever happen across it on a car radio or some public place.

My husband and I lived together in several apartments and houses in different Southern states. First, there was busy, serpentine Jefferson Park Avenue, "JPA," in Charlottesville. We caught the bus at a stop just outside our building and rode to the University of Virginia Library, where we shut ourselves into separate carrels and wrote. Or, he did. I stared out the narrow, floor-to-ceiling window in front of my desk at a giant oak that spread its branches over the lawn below.

Next, we lived on Wild Turkey Lane, a few miles from JPA, isolated in the hills surrounding the valley. The street sign was constantly stolen. Our neighbors were two horses we named for the color of their coats: Blackie and Big Creamy, gentle, noble characters in our inner lives.

Our last address was Butternut Drive, a dead-end loop in a lushly green town in Alabama. My husband landed a tenure-track job teaching poetry, and I worked as an assistant to a professor of acoustics and vibration.

I was ill-suited for my role, as I was for everything, not having yet found myself. My boss, Dr. Crocker, was a charming, world-weary, older man from England.

It really doesn't matter, he'd sometimes say in a dry tone when he was exasperated. But I could sense from a sad undercurrent in his voice that it did matter.

Finding few restaurants up to our personal standards in Auburn, my husband and I learned to cook together. We luxuriated over dinners and much wine, each gaining nearly twenty pounds. Our favorite meals were a cauliflower and potato curry dotted with burst-open mustard seeds, spaghetti in a lush, briny red sauce, creamy chickpea curry spritzed with lemon, and pizza topped with Fontina. I don't remember all the ingredients; I remember smudges on the recipe pages. We made the ones we loved over and over, refrains.

In the first year of a new century, when I met my husband, I didn't view him romantically. He was my professor in a poetry course in the MFA program I attended. Not that, historically, someone being my teacher had prevented me from being obsessed with them. He had a dark Seattle beard and ice-blue eyes that were kind, distant, and a bit merry, and he reminded me of a teddy bear, solid, huggable. I felt a sense of comfort, safety, and playfulness in his presence.

I got to know him slowly. I listened to what he said about poetry and took his advice on my work, which was good advice. In an encouraging way, he let me know that no one understood what the hell was happening in my poems. A painful, important realization.

After classes, our workshop group hung out over beers at the High Desert Brewing Co. in Las Cruces, New Mexico. The following semester, a few of us kept up the ritual of sharing a pitcher and burgers with pepper jack cheese. That's when the feelings came. I became aware of my former mentor in an overwhelming way.

Because I was a student and, at twenty-five, significantly younger, he didn't pursue me. It wouldn't have occurred to him. He'd never dated a younger woman. And he was scrupulous—he wouldn't take such a risk, the kind that could potentially cause him to lose his job and reputation.

On Valentine's Day, I left a heart-shaped, foil-wrapped chocolate with a Post-it that said *Happy V Day* in the cubby that was his faculty mailbox.

THE HAUNT

Around the corner from the Ithaca Commons, at Just A Taste, you could order decadent small plates. There was a courtyard out back with wrought iron furniture and little, windblown trees with silvery leaves or bare, filigree branches next to a bank parking lot, but I usually sat inside at the bar.

The servers needed to descend into the lower level to grab supplies, like cloth napkins, during dinner service. To get to the bathrooms, you walked down a narrow hallway over trap doors. Walking over the black rectangles—cut-out shapes in the floor—felt disconcerting, as if the doors could give way from under you at any moment.

Nicky had been a waiter there for years. *The Ithaca Times* interviewed him when profiling the restaurant, and soon after we met, its readers would vote him Best Waiter in the City. His customers felt genuinely valued and, like me, were drawn to his humble warmth and empathy and sexy, mischievous sparkle.

Everyone who worked at the restaurant was impressive. One of the line cooks, Whitey, played in a band—gorgeously ethereal rock I heard performed live. At The Haunt.

After close, Nicky, the line cooks, and other waitstaff sat at the bar with me. He counted the money, and we all kept drinking and laughing until three a.m., locked inside away from the rest of the world.

On one of those nights—desserts with crème anglaise, candlelight—Nicky slid his arm around my back and squeezed.

His cat-like green eyes, always intently focused, were serious. Worried. *How is your mom doing?*

In my childhood home, people became frighteningly angry, the kind of angry that turned physical at any moment.

You had to be pleasant and hardworking and go with the program, whatever that was. You took orders. You could not voice what you felt or needed. I mean, you could, but that would just make you tremendously aware that what you felt didn't matter and what you needed—your basic, intangible requirements—were impossible.

This is how I describe what I've labeled over the years as abuse. If you expressed disagreement, the response might be a fury of hands beating your shoulders and back, a quick face slap, screaming, being called *ungrateful bitch, selfish, worthless.* Objects like magazines or Rescue Squad equipment thrown at you. Or just thrown. At nothing.

The rest of the time, the atmosphere was cheerful in a tense, high-voltage way, all off-color sarcasm and Howard Stern on the car radio. My mom and stepdad were young. They had a lot of energy and weren't offended by cursing or the mention of sex. They cursed often, expressively. They were also highly organized and responsible. My siblings and I were well-provided for. My mom stacked beautifully wrapped presents under a

Christmas tree that sagged with hundreds of ornaments, enough tinsel and lights to ignite us all. She was a selfless, attuned gift-giver who delivered exactly what you'd wanted, if not something better. On one holiday in the 1980s, I tore the wrappings off not just one, but—overwhelmingly—*two* Cabbage Patch Kids.

When we went to Sandy Hook, my stepfather—an overachiever like my mom—always built a large, intricate sandcastle, using our plastic kiddie pails and tiny shovels to shape towers and turrets. His castles were the envy of every child on the beach who wandered over to splash with us in the moat. For hours, my siblings and I sat below its pointed walls and dug in the chilled, damp sand for shells and tiny crabs. Then as the afternoon faded, high tide rolled in and, bit by bit, washed the whole creation away.

The staff at Just A Taste lived in

a way that I'd never managed. They enjoyed their drama-free lives. Behind the steamed-up plate glass windows looking out on North Aurora Street, a world flourished where they prioritized the right things. Savoring the moments of a decadent meal and peppery, velvety wine, leisure, belly laughs, little topaz flames from candles. Intimate, relaxed.

Then with the careless destructiveness of an explosion, my stepdad— The thing is, I can't tell that story, I've told myself for years. Because it's not mine.

Shortly after my Happy V Day declaration, the man who would become my husband and I went to the High Desert Brewing Co.—just us two. I pitched the idea of having a relationship to him.

He shared his serious reservations about our age and power differential. I debated them. Whatever was between us, I said—the feelings and energy—was like a Mack truck bearing down. He responded with something about it being more like a Pinto. Not our feelings for each other. His confidence about acting on them.

We had sex that night.

In the mornings, he and I read and talked for hours, lounging on his mattress on the floor—recently divorced, he had little furniture—sipping cappuccinos out of red and blue ceramic mugs. This was in a little adobe house in the Chihuahuan Desert, with a turquoise-blue front door.

He may not have had much, but dude had an espresso machine.

Toasted sesame bagels and cream cheese with bits of green olive, a spindly old wooden chair piled with books next to the mattress on the floor, and in a white alcove above it, another stack of *New Yorkers* and poetry volumes blocking the window. Everything I'd ever truly need in the world.

On Saturday nights, Nicky was in a tense mood after waiting on people at the restaurant all week. Sad-angry. *It's padded room time*, he'd say. He had a dramatic way of putting things.

On one of his "padded room" nights, I went out alone, nervous and guilty and giddily hopeful, to The Haunt, a nightclub set next to a swampy inlet to Cayuga Lake. I'd been there a decade earlier in my college days, when The Haunt hosted weekly epic 80s nights. You could barely move in the press of dancing bodies.

Earlier that afternoon, I'd gotten a shock: a message left on my answering machine from Ryan's best friend. I'd met Ryan when I'd first moved back to Ithaca, but the relationship had been short-lived. Ryan couldn't stop talking about me, Manny complained. It was driving him crazy.

I'd last seen Ryan in his cave-like living room. The room contained only a trunk he'd taken to Iraq that he used as a desk to do homework on and two hideous brown couches. We sat on separate ones. The thin, paneled walls around us shook, and outside, snow gusted and trucks slammed by on Route 96. The room was where he'd dumped me.

Manny said he and Ryan would be at The Haunt that night, and could I please stop by and say hi so Manny wouldn't have to keep hearing about how Ryan missed me and had screwed up and wished he could go back in time and do everything differently.

I gushed this news to friends, a couple who pointed out that this seemed like a junior-high type of strategy. It hadn't occurred to me that Ryan had orchestrated Manny's call—exploding four months of silence between us.

Nor did I care.

A few hours after Manny's phone message, I stood at chest-level to Ryan in the crowd at The Haunt. Though I was with Nicky, I dreamed about Ryan. Now I had to tilt my head back to see his face, so near was he.

His gray-blue eyes glittered and his short reddish hair, buzzed on the sides for the National Guard, looked lighter, gold-tipped. The small change was a reminder of how far he'd been from me.

He leaned down close to my ear—it felt like a spotlight turned on deep in my chest.

After some nervous catching up, we slow danced outside on the patio above the sluggish inlet. *You and me, and no one else*, he said, his breath Redbull and vodka.

The next day, I phoned Nicky from the cordless in my apartment. He was blindsided.

From the next room, my mom, recently made homeless, heard my half of the breakup. I'm *crazy*, I'll *regret this choice.* Her feedback wasn't helpful.

Earlier that same week, I'd dropped by Nicky's house out of the blue with a bouquet of lilacs from a florist. He was always orchestrating such romantic, spontaneous moments for me. Once, when we met for a Sunday drive, he presented me with a vintage dress made of a shimmery, garnet-colored fabric. It was a little loose on me but magical.

When I knocked on the door, Nicky was sanding banisters in the stairwell and wore a dust mask, his eyebrows gray with wood shavings. He turned the loud sander off, pushed the mask up, and noticed the flowers. His face lit with happy surprise.

On our first dates, Ryan and I had shot pool at a dive bar decorated with fake palm trees to resemble a Caribbean island. We caught the Johnny Dowd band—introspective, ambient folk-rock—at an old pub called Chapter House on a cobblestone street near Cornell. At Watkins Glen Gorge, we wandered around a maze of rock paths above shimmering loops of water that rushed below, as they had since the gorge was carved by a glacier thousands of years before.

"Just Moved Back to Ithaca," Ryan's ad on Craigslist had been titled. *So did I!* I'd replied—on impulse. I'd been looking for jobs after my move from Alabama and stumbled on the personals. I hoped to find someone to do things with—and that I wouldn't be serial-killed. I wasn't looking to date.

Neither Ryan nor I had posted a photo, but we somehow recognized each other at the rendezvous spot: the overhang outside Collegetown Bagels. He was over six feet tall, athletic, and shy. Respectful. Mid-twenties but could pass for younger. His buzzed red hair seemed to be a darker, earthy color on that first meeting, like he blended with the night air.

From the bagel place, we walked to Cornell Cinema in the rain to see a documentary, "Searching for the Wrong-Eyed Jesus." Ryan didn't use an umbrella: a stubborn lack of care was typical of him, I'd learn.

I gushed in my journal, debriefing later, *I can't believe I went out with a 25 yr old soldier boy! & yet I found his rain-soaked physicality appealing.* In the theater, sexual magnetism emanated from him in hot waves.

Ryan was five years younger than me, around my little brother's age. He'd recently left active duty in the army, started college, and began working at the returns counter at Home Depot. He was, endearingly, slogging his way through a list of one hundred greatest literary classics, a project he'd started the previous year in Iraq. He was stalled in *Heart of Darkness.*

If I could have dreamed up someone the opposite of my husband, Ryan would be the guy. Quiet and mysterious. Wild.

Really, this isn't what Ryan was like, but for years, I thought it was.

He'd spent a year in Baghdad, where he was under shell fire twenty-four hours a day and his friends were blown up by IEDs, turned to what soldiers called pink mist. He'd grown up poor in the tiny village of Dryden, outside of Ithaca. His father was gone, due to a rare neurological disease. And his mom, who was not yet old, suffered with serious health and mental health diagnoses and lived, precariously it seemed, in low-income housing for seniors. Above everything—I now understand—Ryan was painfully ambitious. He wanted an orderly, stable family life.

My stepfather and mom separated abruptly, as I had from my husband. The following two years would be a whirl of terms like "arson" and "TRO"—temporary restraining order—and multiple, fabricated lawsuits brought against my mom.

At first, my parents still lived under one roof. I called my stepdad and begged him to move out. Instead, he filed domestic violence reports with the local police—even though he traveled by airplane for work and was away Monday through Friday and my mom didn't want to see him on weekends.

After months of reports, when the burden of proof needed to issue a TRO could not be met, a judge issued a protective order instead. My mom wasn't permitted to be in the house when my stepdad was home. Each weekend, she had to find somewhere to go, leaving behind not only over twenty pets but also Biggie. The many details of her mother's care, the frequent ER visits, were my mom's immense, anxious responsibility.

For seven years, my disabled grandmother lived in a hospital bed in a room pristinely equipped for her medical needs near my parents' master suite. Biggie's room had a vaulted ceiling and cozy, electric fireplace, and my mom, ever a maximalist, had brightened it with knickknacks and mementos from Biggie's house. Every bit of wall or shelf space was covered with decorative plates, statuettes, family photos. There were special-edition Barbies, perfect in the box, and life-sized porcelain dolls that scared me.

Pop Pop's wooden rocking chair sat

facing Biggie. When I was a child, he'd sat in the chair like a boss next to his wife's smaller rocker, and we watched *Columbo* together in their den. Now when I visited Biggie, I settled on his brown, corduroy cushion, next to the metal bars of her bed.

She was always lightly made up, wearing fuchsia matte lipstick that smelled like flowers when I hugged her, and fully dressed in rhinestone-bedizened blouses and sweaters, slacks, and fashion scarves.

One Monday when my mom returned to the mansion after her weekend shut-out, Biggie was gone. Without notification, my stepdad had sent my ninety-two-year-old grandmother and her caregiver, Kathleen, to live with Uncle John. In California.

Alone in the cavernous, empty house, in anguish, my mom set fire to clothing my stepdad had left in their dryer. In a large, stainless steel dog food bowl, she torched new men's bikini underwear with sayings like "Hot Tamale" splashed colorfully over the crotch.

LIZ GREEN

My stepdad had my mom arrested, locked in a mental hospital, and thrown out of their home. For a year and a half—until the mansion sold—he held her belongings hostage, every item of her clothing. My grandparents' furniture. And though he didn't follow through on it, he told my brother to inform our mother he'd dump the baby cats and her two frail, aging dogs at a shelter.

Everywhere we'd lived, my husband and I kept what we called "The Big Board": a few sheets of yellow legal paper held by a magnet onto the refrigerator, on which we'd write down the other person's utterances. *Rickets is my favorite nutrition-based disease. You know to always dock ten minutes off of everything I say.*

I was progressing through my second MFA, having transferred from New Mexico State University to a low-residency program in order to follow my husband's career. Completing the degree was a glorious ordeal, and he supported me emotionally—I'd become an insecure wreck as my poems became due—and financially.

He was the one who paid our rent and other bills. He leaped into action after dinner to wash the dishes, while I lounged with my glass of wine. He cleaned. He took the recycling outside. I wasn't good at any of those things, meaning uninterested. I spent much of each day sobbing in my office—we each had our own, at opposite ends of the house—because of pressure I felt to produce good poems for the brilliantly inspiring mentors in my program. And loneliness. We scorned little Auburn, a football-obsessed town, and had few friends.

Why had I left him? Why did I think there was something more to be had than our life together, ideal for two writers? Boredom, longing, feeling trapped and alone: these feelings, recurrent during our two-year marriage, became my reasons. I'd left because I was impulsive and didn't know what I wanted.

The couples' therapist we saw, a woman with a heavy Southern twang, hated when I expressed an emotion and always took my husband's side—the rational side. I felt like a freak in those sessions.

You're moody and depressed and hard to deal with, my husband said during one of our breakup talks. An assessment that haunts me.

I alternately feel a great current of strength and energy and at-one-ness, I wrote in a journal the summer I left him. *And as if I'm crazy, immature, a panicky feeling. Like I'm making a big mistake.*

I'd had no experience living with a romantic partner or being in a committed relationship. Before I met my husband, my love life had consisted of being the other woman or yearning for physically or emotionally distant men who didn't reciprocate.

As a child, I'd lived some scary moments, and deep down, underneath the Mack truck feeling I'd once enthused about to my husband, I believed other people were dangerous and should be kept at bay. I trusted nothing.

THE HAUNT

There are people who are dead who would love to have a hole in their sweatpants—this line from The Big Board made it into one of my poems.

Why did I need an intensity of feeling I was aware existed but had never experienced?

Shortly after Biggie's death, I emailed my stepfather.

Dear Dad,

I am sure you are surprised to hear from me and probably don't want to hear from me, since we have not spoken in years. I know you're aware of the reason for my silence, the lack of a respectful, cordial relationship between you and Mom. When that changes, I will be more than happy to connect again, if you want to.

I am writing now with a favor to ask, which I hope you will consider honoring, if you ever cared for me. As I think you did. Of course, it's about Biggie's funeral. I am not writing to call you the bad guy, to say you have no place at the funeral, or to discuss what has gone on between you and my mom. I am saying this: She isn't ready to see you in person yet. The loss of a parent has to be the hardest time in someone's life (as I'm sure you know—I was so sorry to hear about your mom). My mom is taking the death pretty hard. Since she is legally not allowed to talk to you, I am asking you to respect her wishes—and mine—and please do not attend the mass or viewings. You knew Biggie for many years and you both cared a lot for each other, it's true, and I'm sure you want to say goodbye too. I think there are other ways that you could show your respect and support without being there in person...

And so on. He never responded.

The staff at Just A Taste sometimes held celebratory events when the restaurant closed for a holiday, but I never went to one because I'd left Nicky to go back to Ryan. When we were a couple, Nicky had told me, rapturously, about how they'd all gather at Whitey and Elise's stylish, hip house in the countryside.

Elise was a waitress and one of the most beautiful people I've ever seen, with flawless skin. I'd just found out I had a permanent skin condition. During that first year of my separation—and my parents'—a dermatologist in Syracuse diagnosed rosacea. My face was registering all my stress, sadness, and existential terror. My skin was blotchy, pores enlarging. Flare-ups of broken veins and small bumps, pustules, on my cheeks and nose were caused by everything that brought relief from my feelings: drinking, spicy or rich foods, heat or cold, chocolate, crying, sunlight.

Elise was gracious, with perfect manners, and she had a wry smile, as if she were aware of things I could never be—and was amused about that. Her relationship with Whitey seemed like a dreamworld of fun, full of friends and vintage cookware and cocktail parties everyone loved to look back on.

When Ryan and I first met, he thought I made him wait a long time—six weeks—before we began having sex. More sex than I'd had in years. It was like a lighthearted sport but also weirdly tender, on a deep, intuitive soul level.

I'd lie awake next to him afterwards, giddy, until pink light touched the row of button-down plaid shirts hanging in his doorless closet.

One night when we'd been out drinking, I let him drive my Honda Civic at 100 mph on a twisty country road, the car fishtailing wildly. When I was with Ryan, my whole life was confetti that I was tossing in the air, not caring where it would land.

Two years into the separation from my husband, I received a large manila envelope in the mail from a lawyer he'd apparently hired. Divorce papers named me as "defendant." They were written as if in my husband's voice. Over and over on the pages, one statement was repeated: *The child is not mine.*

Though I should have been expecting this, I wasn't: my private, unplanned condition blared on every page. My husband usually sent me cards, packages, and handwritten notes from Auburn that were signed *Love, C.*, on yellow, lined paper. Pictures of the new cat lounging on "our" porch, who looked like our sweet Maine coon, a Zen fluff we used to pet while she dozed on those sunny boards.

Was it true that I couldn't be my deep-down, real self with him? That self was cranky and neurotic and wanted things that made no sense to my husband. Like for him to pretend to be a cop and arrest me. I'd gotten up the nerve to voice this desire, once—and was not encouraged.

Our first summer apart, he'd gone to

Europe. It was a trip we'd have relished together as foodie snobs who became excited about museums. He sent me mementos. Glossy Kodaks taken in European capitals. A large, broadside-type card of a letter "E," for my name, in the style of old illuminated manuscripts, with tendrils and swoops of brilliant color. A postcard of the death mask of our idol, poet John Keats.

On a level we didn't discuss but that was present in the paranoid, detached wording of the documents, we were both a grieving shitshow mess. As most divorcing people are. There was no chance we'd process our mutual loss with each other. My pregnancy, shortly after Ryan and I got back together, made that loss permanent.

> Ay, in the very temple of Delight
> Veil'd Melancholoy has her sovran
>   shrine…

I knew the "Ode on Melancholy" by

heart and used to recite it to my husband over dinner.

At Keats's two-hundred-year-old grave in Rome, my husband had taken a selfie in a periwinkle-blue T-shirt. The shirt's color set off his piercing Norwegian eyes that used to try to reach mine—kindly, inquisitively—when I was upset and shut down.

I've seen this picture on various websites since then, as my ex's success as a published poet has cemented. When I break down and Google him.

You'll need this if you ever remarry, he emailed about the divorce decree, still trying to be helpful to me, as he always had. A fact I find excruciating.

At restaurants or wine bars, sitting alone with a book—or these days, iPhone—I feel sheltered and also supported. It's a guilty pleasure: someone waiting on me, even if it's basically theater. Another person going out of their way, pretending to care about what would make me feel good, what wine might unfold lusciously with notes of rose and chocolate, shepherding me into pleasures because, underpaid, they live on tips.

Good waitstaff know how to connect emotionally but in a way that doesn't intrude. It's based on instinct, making calculations and taking risks. When to approach the table and talk to their customer, when to bring this or that delicacy out, when to check on the diner. How much conversation to make, what kind of mood to project? What mood can the lone customer handle?

Sometimes when I was blissed out at Just A Taste, my mom, who'd been discharged against medical advice from a psych ward, was alone at my apartment. Set up in my bed with a "husband" pillow and reading a true crime biography, she was safe and comfy. Or so I hoped.

Unmoored from everything and almost everyone, she told me I should definitely go out, have fun.

I'd picked her up from at least one facility, in Connecticut, where I signed the discharge papers. I had to swear she wasn't suicidal and assume all responsibility.

Dear Dad,

You haven't responded to my email yet. I was speaking from the heart, trying to prevent a potentially explosive situation, so I'm sorry not to have heard a positive response from you. I found out that Mom spoke to her lawyer, wondering about the repercussions of direct contact with you if that should happen next week, and he told her that under no circumstances was she to be in the same place as you. He advised her to notify the funeral parlor director and show him your picture so that, should you show up at the funeral parlor, the church, or the cemetery, you will be denied entrance. If it becomes necessary, the police will be called to remove you. I'm writing this as a courtesy because I don't want there to be an unpleasant and unnecessary scene at my grandmother's services. Since you have a restraining order against my mother, you've created the conditions that are forbidding you to attend. You have left her no choice but to follow her attorney's advice, as it is not an option for her to be arrested at her mother's funeral.

I'm truly sorry—and uncomfortable—to have to give you this news. That it has come to this.

From my spot at the bar at Just A Taste, it was my habit to look up at a row of antique radios displayed on a high shelf. Nicky loved to restore old things, lavish them with care and attention, and he'd brought them back to mint condition.

Nicky put a lot of TLC into the old radios, their festive colors reminiscent of nail polish or candy. I loved the turquoise, a light, wistful oceanic blue. There was also the rose-pink I favored. There were white, red, black, banana-yellow radios, their colors attached to a hierarchy of monetary value. The passionate red was the most sought after.

On Sundays, I often went with him on his expeditions to the many nearby antique shops, searching for rare objects that had been neglected and abandoned. I automatically assumed that what mattered to him should be significant to me, and I should emulate his preferences. I was this way with friends and lovers. Like an apprentice training to become a real person with approved-of desires, opinions, and values. What I believed or wanted fluctuated, highly inconveniently—and still does—as in a kaleidoscope where reflected fragments seem to make different patterns.

Nicky and I strolled slowly through these dim antique malls—so much to look at on every surface. He taught me about Bakelite, a plastic beautiful as glass used for dishes and jewelry, and Czechoslovakian End-of-Day

Glass. Pieces of missing contexts. Who'd owned each discarded object, what were their lives like, and where were they now?

To Nicky, love meant repair.

I can still see the garnet-colored dress, dream-like, hanging from the chandelier in Nicky's bedroom. *Maybe one day you'll remember what it was like being treated well,* he said once. *Or then again, maybe you won't.*

With brutal suddenness, after almost thirty years together, my stepdad broke up with my mom. They were both still in the McMansion, and he was openly dating the other woman. I phoned him. I was so nervous: I never called him to *talk*. But even though we'd never had a close relationship, I'd believed, maybe wrongly, that he and I were the most reasonable people in our home. Compared to my operatically emotional mother. I rang his work cell and said something like, *Uh, could you move out of the house*?

I intervened in their divorce a few times. I'm not sure if I was actually asked to. Or if I felt it was expected of me, the oldest of four siblings, to mediate. Or that doing so was a display of appropriate loyalty to my once strong, secure mom.

My inner feelings vacillated: *I feel so sad and irritated, I come home and it's not festive, it's stressful and scary*. Then, *I'm going to be compassionate to my mom, I see that she's suffering and I have to do something.*

I'd been keeping the peace my whole life, gauging others' moods and needs and adjusting to show them what they wanted from me. It was confusing. Exhausting. My Uncle John called me "the little diplomat," so over-the-top was my false cheer. To those places, pets, and people around whom I experience my true self, I formed special, doomed attachments.

My stepdad said he couldn't afford to move, not even to a cheap, temporary place, as I suggested. His response was as baffling as it was untrue. He worked a consulting job in the software programming field and jetted all over the country. He parked his Lexus under a sign in the driveway that read "Aikido Master Parking Only."

Nicky loved the Art Deco era. For the rest of my life, should I glimpse a lamp with a particular base, the slender, evocative statuette of a nude, I'll know it's Art Deco. The solitary, female figure holding a small globe glowing red, orange, cobalt, or emerald.

Early in our relationship, Ryan and I had planned to meet up for New Year's Eve. That day as I waited to hear from him, water leaked into my apartment from an upstairs neighbor's toilet. I felt my mood slip from excitedly hopeful to anxious to outright panicked.

Eventually, the building maintenance guy came by my unit and carved a gaping, soggy hole in the bathroom ceiling—a little cavern of sheetrock and pipes and wires I would have to look at for days. When he took off to ring in the holiday at home with his wife and boys, I was in a state that felt entirely beyond control or intervention. Anguished about Ryan's silence and our vague, ruined plans, about myself, and about everything ever.

When I was a kid, people angry at me or hitting me triggered this state. I flip-flopped between feeling like part of my family, albeit also an outsider not truly understood or appreciated, and being exiled, sad and scared and full of rage.

After I left my husband, this exile-state became a more and more frequent experience. Like there was now a trade-off: I could be repressed but safe and secure. Or feel passionate and abandoned.

Ryan and I had been dating for just three months. I still smiled the entire time I drove up Route 96 to his tiny, desolate, shithole apartment building. His apartment was almost next door to an antique mall that Nicky and I would later frequent, a coincidence that quietly devastated me when Nicky drove us past Ryan's place.

A few nights after the New Year's when Ryan never called—still no word from him—I let a stranger try to fuck me in the tiny bathroom at Micawber's. Then, in distress, I ran the two miles back to my apartment blackout drunk. The sidewalks were icy, and I tripped, flew briefly, landed, and sprawled forward, shredding deep layers of skin off both palms. All through January, I wore embarrassing large bandages over my hands.

About the abuse I grew up with, the deep, permanent loneliness: I don't like the idea of naming anyone specifically, who did what. It would be false to separate out one thread of the story, as if everything that surrounds it, the larger context—even beyond what one can reasonably imagine—doesn't matter. My great-grandfather, who'd emigrated from Italy when just a teen, and who beat his wife and four sons, whistling at the dinner table. The woods on either side of Rick Road, when my mom and stepdad moved there. A vast tangle.

When I became Nicky's girlfriend, I drank for free, because that's what happens when you date someone who works in a restaurant. I've dated a few—a chef, a front-of-house manager, bartenders. I wasn't motivated by that benefit, but it's definitely lagniappe, meaning a nice little somethin' extra, as people in Louisiana, where I now live, say.

Before Nicky and I went out, I would hit on him when he waited on me. We shared our ages. His answer was: *How old do you want me to be?* He was a decade my senior.

At his workplace, so many times they all flow together, I'm sipping a globe of Malbec, waiting for my tapas. I'm looking up at Nicky's radios. Below them, a glass case. I'd never seen anything like it before then. Inside are wines on tap. The bartender just opens a spigot, and voila, wine flows out. A good sight because the first sip soothes the edges of my anxiety and regret.

The food at Just A Taste was served in cozy white oval dishes. Garlic-braised greens with tomatoes, walnuts, sherry vinegar, and Stilton blue cheese, deep-fried Russet wedges with chipotle aioli, salt cod fritters with arugula. Despite the fact that Nicky was older than me, which had always been my preference, it was around that time, after leaving my professor husband, when I started liking younger men—a sea change I seemed to have no say in.

Now, at age forty-seven, I'd say that it's possible to access certain feelings or truths through another person. Like they're a radio transmitting something that awakens part of you—your own ability to notice when your most intimate preferences are valued, magnified. You can inhabit them temporarily.

I last saw Nicky in New Orleans fourteen years ago. Ryan and I and our two-year-old daughter had just moved there for him to attend law school.

Ryan had happy-cried openly when our girl was born. He held my right knee for almost three hours while I pushed, blubbering, terrified to my core. *This baby should have been born hours ago,* the midwife said.

At the time, I earned little editing for the Buddhist press and the journal *Rationality & Society*. I loved book culture but not editing. All I was good at was introspecting, and I hadn't figured out how to make a living at it.

Ryan was finishing his bachelor's at Cornell after he'd transferred from a community college, a step in his lifelong plan.

We were struggling to establish ourselves as adults, with huge pressure as new parents to fill gaps that required larger support structures. I wouldn't understand this until much later. Ryan suffered from PTSD from the Iraq War. I wasn't the person who could soothe and restore him. Or myself. Or anyone.

We fought constantly, ugly, vicious griping about care of our daughter, each of us feeling that the other wasn't doing enough. We had no nearby family help and few resources. We screamed *fucking fuck you!* at each other in the Wegman's parking lot.

The transformation beyond recognition of what's been most important, at the center of one's life—I'm so familiar with this story.

Eventually, I could no longer survive with Ryan and I left him, soon after we arrived in New Orleans.

Nicky visited because I was single again.

THE HAUNT

I exposed him to scabies. The doctor I'd seen for the inflamed skin between my fingers, the red trails on my arms and legs, told me the problem was either eczema or heat rash. It was not. It was a highly contagious affliction in which microscopic organisms burrow into the skin and live there. Eventually the body is covered in scabs that itch every second like wildfire.

Nicky's mother lived in New Orleans. Probably still does, for all I know.

He called her "Mom." He never said *my mom.* Just *Mom*, like it was an illustrious title yet also intensely warm and personal. She'd had Nicky when very young and a single parent, as I'd also be—permanently. Ryan would be the last person, besides my daughter, I'd roll the dice and live with.

Nicky and Mom were best friends. From the outside they shared an almost romantic bond, the worshipful merging Nicky felt with her—and also projected toward any woman he became close to. I couldn't handle that.

Mom owned and ran a Bed and Breakfast in the French Quarter. You must be powerful to own anything in the Quarter, the oldest, most romantic part of the city, like an annex of Europe or the Caribbean.

Nicky and I drank many absinthe cocktails in Pirate's Alley during his trip and fucked nostalgically in a four-poster bed in a candlelit room in Mom's B and B. A Creole Cottage-style building, the B and B coincidentally, eerily sat directly across Barracks Street from the attic apartment that Ryan had recently moved to.

A few weeks later, Ryan and I had to rush our toddler to Children's Hospital. She had pneumonia. The staff also diagnosed the scabies—maybe contracted at her daycare, they speculated—and quarantined all three of us.

I had no job. I had scabs caused by hostile microorganisms covering me.

For a while, after our reunion, Nicky and I exchanged long emails spilling our intimate news. His finding of a tin cornice for his kitchen, after years of searching. My two numb, highly functional weeks on Lexapro. Ongoing attempts to rid myself and my daughter of scabies with Permethrin, the main ingredient in flea meds for dogs. Then neem oil, which smelled like rotten crushed garlic. Then sulfur soap.

I'd soon start dating a playwright who worked as a chef at the Delachaise, a train-car-shaped, twinkling-white-light-festooned wine bar in my new neighborhood. When I ordered a Malbec, the bartenders served it in an adorable, petite glass decanter I leisurely tipped over my wine glass.

According to our letters, Nicky visited New Orleans twice in the months after his first trip. I have no memory of him ever coming back.

On my barstool at Just A Taste, during my era as a regular, looking at the shelf of antique radios, I'm in this ambient, drifting frame of mind. Anchored, but also daydreaming. One of my favorite ways to feel. In the state where I'm tethered to the earth by featherlight cords that are the glass of Riesling, the goose-fat fries. Like I'm present and I like being here, but I'm also not here because I feel so chill-happy that I'm flowing and being in ease. That's where I would be, if I could define home now. I would just be *in ease.*

My stepfather and I now follow each other on Instagram. He and his wife—that same woman—live somewhere in the Florida Keys, having ended up in the South, like me. Based on his content, they're deeply involved in feeding and spaying feral cats, in transporting puppies for a rescue group.

I never see them. I met his wife once, a decade ago, at a gathering at my stepsister's old house in Trenton. Late middle-aged, matronly, with a bowl haircut reminiscent of the Beatles, the wife appeared ordinary and harmless and was perfectly nice to me the way a schoolteacher is to small children.

My stepdad texts me on my birthday, eight days before his. Or when another hurricane descends and blacks out my city.

New baby not fully open, he posts, with a close-up of a blossoming lilac branch, I guess, from his yard.

In the final analysis, a phrase my calm grandmother used to say, in my moments of looking back from some imaginary endpoint I have yet to arrive at, should I feel regret?

When Ryan returned from Baghdad, before we met, he'd settled in a rundown apartment building on Route 96. In the common hallway hung a framed photograph of a red rose, beads of water on its velvety petals. My eyes went to the cheesy, splayed flower each time I passed it, up the stairs, heart-poundingly anxious and anticipatory, to knock on Ryan's door.

He always muttered *Come in*, and though I knew the door was unlocked, I knocked anyway, scared to assume that level of intimacy, that I could just show up and enter. His voice sounded deadened and bored, which I enjoyed. The contrast between his apparent lack of enthusiasm to see me as compared to, later in bed, his sexy, reverent gasps of *Oh God* and *Oh shit*. Or the bottomless desire I felt versus the fact that I saw him only once a week and had no idea what he was doing the rest of the time.

We slept under his velvety throw blanket. That is, he slept. I was too happy to sleep. He said a friend, an Iraqi man, had gifted him the blanket. Its violet color, and the rendition of a single, huge rose embroidered on it, embarrassed Ryan's sense of masculinity. But not too much, because he seemed poignantly proud of the memento.

A year later, after I'd had and lost a lovely and comforting life with Nicky, I helped Ryan pack his few boxes. We were moving into a nicer place in downtown Ithaca, because I'd insisted on somewhere cute. It even had a stained-glass window in the bathroom. I was eight months pregnant.

I fully intended to steal the photo in the hallway of Ryan's building, the red rose, saddened at the thought of never seeing it again. At the last minute I changed my mind, wanting to allow the picture to mean something else, one day, to another person.

The bar at Just A Taste featured a painting of a bull. The bull sits at the same bar where I sat, waiting for Nicky's shift to end, an almost empty glass in front of the creature that contained fragments of ice in some bitter spirit—I imagined.

I was constantly trying to understand why that painting moved me. It was just a bull gazing distantly, a rocks glass before him. The earthy brushstrokes, oranges and browns and reds, a little transgressive green. The vibe warm, sexy, world-weary.

I felt connected to the painter's impressionistic vision and to the bull, gloomy and masculine, contemplative, a little punk.

I learned the bull was a portrait of Coxy, a line cook who once worked at the restaurant. I'd peripherally known him. Years earlier, my then-housemate, Melanie, had been deeply invested in him; she'd had to get an abortion. He hadn't hidden his fuming resentment about escorting her to the appointment, the last time they'd ever seen each other. Nicky hated Coxy. He was a drunk, Nicky said, an asshole to women. It had been years since the guy had set foot in the place, but the portrait still hung on the wall. I sat across from it, the bull facing me, looking at nothing discernable, anywhere, and I looked back at him.

You are alone, I felt as a kid, in my worst moments. No one's going to rescue you, no one cares. What you thought was real wasn't, and what you thought was good has vanished. Had it ever existed?

At the time of her death, Biggie had long been half-paralyzed. Confined to a wheelchair or hospital bed and in need of a special van to go anywhere. Her beautiful stiff right arm cradled in a sling. For eight years.

It was a lot at once: that she was gone, that I'd been barred from Just A Taste, which had helped me hold myself together.

In my early life, my mom had been the powerful being at the center of everyone's universe, and my stepdad orbited her. I may not have liked it, her absolute authority, but it was something I *knew*.

After we broke up, Nicky sent me emails about how he'd been vomiting ever since, he couldn't sleep, and his housemate, who'd also been my friend, had to peel him off the floor where he lay heartbroken.

It hadn't been intentional, my effect on this man. I could never give him what he needed from me. It had been better to release him, the way I've had to do for myself. The way it's been done to me. Brutally and for the best. A fiancé, places I've loved, jobs. Go find what you need. It's not here. Maybe it's somewhere.

Back when my friend Melanie was still with Coxy, the line cook/bull, she and I were walking in the Fall Creek neighborhood, and she showed me where he lived. Nearby, from North Tioga Street, a little footbridge crossed Cascadilla Creek. Slender metal railings ran alongside the stream, and old-fashioned streetlamps illuminated the pedestrian walkway. A large blue house sat adjacent to the walkway. Coxy lived there, with roommates.

Melanie pointed out his bedroom on the second floor, perched over the little channel of rushing water, a room made almost entirely of windows.

In New Orleans, I went back to school and became a therapist, and I have been in this role for over a decade. I stay alert for moments of somebody feeling good about themselves or their life, making a sudden connection between conflicting or vastly different things, inside, that brings relief, and the universe sings.

Throughout my childhood, my stepfather learned to play difficult songs on the baby grand piano that dominated the front room of our house in Fords, down the stairwell from my bedroom. Scott Joplin's "Ragtime" and the sublime "Rhapsody in Blue" by Gershwin. For years, I heard the same brief scraps. Struck keys sounded like ice cracking. Repeated chords floated up the stairs again and again. Stumbling, reiterating fragments, mistakes.

After Melanie pointed them out, I felt strangely drawn to those windows over Cascadilla Creek. When I passed by alone, it was as if I got a hit of whatever she'd had, nights in an undertow of fucking and losing yourself in a room the moonlight flooded.

Like a stalker, I stared up at Coxy's windows. They were impossible to see into. Reflected light ever shifting, minute to minute. The sound of the creek slipping past over rocks.

You grow up in a mess of emotional truths impossible to understand from your own limited perspective. The pain and beauty of generations ago, other countries—somehow still present—that your cells were swimming in since before you were born.

When she wasn't staying with me in Ithaca, my mom called from public phones. It stressed me out. The psych nurses had taken her purse and socks away, and her feet were cold. *If I could just press a button and not exist anymore, I would*, she said once.

Since moving to New Orleans, I've visited Ithaca twice to check on the storage unit I still have there. Bits of a self scattered. It's too expensive to hire movers to transport the contents I can't let go of. Biggie's dining room furniture. Her table, its wood a smooth, blondish hue. I remember it lavishly decorated with holiday dishes, the leaves in place so more plates and people could fit.

No longer banned from Just A Taste, I stopped in and chat-flirted with Nicky. Many of the same people were still working there, a decade later. He and I didn't get involved. He was living with someone. Unlike me, he was happy.

A few miles outside of Ithaca, where Nicky's friends Whitey and Elise hosted the staff parties, countryside undulated vaguely, poetically, in every direction. Hills composed of layers of greens—russets and golds in the fall. If you owned a house there, as the golden couple did, you "had land." Once dairy farms proliferated in the area, but even by the mid-1990s when I attended college nearby, many had fallen into deep, gothic neglect. Remnants of barns and rusted equipment sunk into the ground.

I picture a velvety green lawn, Whitey and Elise's, stretching into the distance. A swanky patio setup, everybody drinking, sharing inside jokes. Transporting music playing. The life I aspired to but never achieved. There are only those moments in an atmospheric restaurant, someplace where my senses are serenaded and lulled, and the pleasurable conditions seem as though they can extend luxuriously into the future.

After the underwear-burning incident, my mom was ejected from her life. She was in and out of mental hospitals, in a crisis state that had flared up, initially, a few years before my stepdad left her.

In her early fifties, she'd been in the prime of a highly accomplished, successful career she enjoyed, working as a systems engineer for a telecommunications giant, when everyone at the company started getting axed. One hundred and twenty-five thousand employees were reduced to twenty-five thousand. In my mom's group of one hundred twenty-five people, four remained. Including her. She was that good.

With two master's degrees—English and computer science—my mom had always been what she and I both referred to as "frighteningly competent." As compared to me: perennially spaced out, in a family of hardworking tech savants. *Your father is one of the most brilliant engineers in the Western world,* Uncle John once joked to me, *and you can't operate a toaster.*

Anyone at my mom's company post-layoffs viciously competed to oust the others, leveraging personal connections and withholding vital information from colleagues who, left in the dark about the work the group was doing, were officially cut.

One night, my stepfather, who never called me, phoned the yellow house where I lived with my husband on a quiet, dead-end street.

Mom's in the loony bin.

There were hundreds of women in there with me, my mom said recently about the state mental hospital for the criminally insane, where she was committed after the "arson" for nearly a month. *And none of them got released except me.*

Sitting at the bar in Just A Taste is feeling wonderfully at home. Not only there. A number of restaurants, bars, and cafés over the years have been a refuge. Places where you're a guest and an observer, where you don't belong.

Do you remember the sex machine? my mom texts from the Lehigh Valley in Pennsylvania, where she lives in her own house on a busy street.

We go back and forth, with her thinking I know what she's referring to. Turns out she's talking about an exercise contraption she once had, on which the handlebars and pedals propelled you in an up-and-down motion.

You kids labeled the machine…Ha ha ha.

In our long-distance relationship, weird emojis and LOLs are our love language.

Recently I had her howling by texting a pic of me from my wedding twenty years ago.

The hairstylist she and I had gone to on the morning of the wedding put our hair in cornrows for some reason. We're Italian American, with fine hair. *My ears look really prominent*, I captioned the pic, the nicest thing I will ever be able to say about how I looked.

My mom had ripped her braids out in the car. I was running late to my own ceremony. At the Washington Crossing Inn, in the front row of folding chairs, under the fluttering white tent hastily erected due to torrential rain, Biggie cried in her wheelchair. She wore the same white, sparkly, sequined pantsuit that she would be interred in, five years later. Biggie adored bling.

Both my stepdad and Bio-Dad attended. My father guided me down the aisle. My stepdad stood and recited a passage from my favorite book, *The Lone Pilgrim* by the late Laurie Colwin—a kindred soul, who wrote tenderly about "nursery food" and family and a person's inner freedom.

While saying our vows, which included the promise, "I will not engage in any shenanigans," my ex-husband wept. I didn't.

The river overflowed its banks that cold June day.

About my hair on my only wedding day: *How the fuck did that even happen?* my mom texted. The question could be applied to much more.

For a long time after my marriage ended, when I went to a Blockbuster, I instantly spotted videos my ex-husband would love. Foreign, film noir. At parties, I felt in my throat the little, annoyed groan/sigh he used to subtly make for my benefit whenever, at some social event, we were trapped by an acquaintance who talked too much.

When I was a child, sometimes the rage that came at me relented more quickly than I'd expected. It was as if whatever had just happened hadn't happened. I was back in the other person's good graces. Everything was okay.

On Sundays, Nicky drove us all over the Finger Lakes region in his maroon Volvo station wagon. His Labrador and soul mate, Ruby, came with us. Her shiny black head nudged into the front seat between him and me, irritating me. We went to antique shops, yes, but more. The waterfalls in tiny Ludlowville, where he'd once lived. Ice cream stands near Seneca Lake. I felt young, free, that I was living a less complicated life. Supported within what was meaningful to him.

I was just living. Rather than missing what is gone, a missing that will not stop.

Near Lake Geneva, we often passed an old abandoned military base where albino deer lived. I'd never known that these otherworldly creatures existed, and I imagined them as trapped there, inside the barbed wire fencing. But how or why had this happened? Sometimes I'd glimpse just one behind the fence, a surprising, lonely flash.

ACKNOWLEDGMENTS

My deepest gratitude goes to Peg Alford Pursell for her brilliant, empathic editorial vision and support, and to Roxanne Guiney and the team at WTAW Press. For all of their care in fully realizing this project, I am moved and thankful. The PhD program in creative writing at the University of Louisiana at Lafayette provided essential space, time, and inspiration to write. Thank you, especially, to Charles Richard for his wonderful feedback and encouragement. For her support of this work and many others, heartfelt thanks to Linda Michele, my mother.

ABOUT THE AUTHOR

Liz Green's nonfiction has been featured in *The Hunger*, *Fourth Genre*, *The Woolf*, *Bright Flash Literary Review*, *Bending Genres,* and *The Opiate.* She received a PhD in English from the University of Louisiana at Lafayette, where she won the Dr. James H. Wilson / Paul T. Nolan Creative Writing Award in Drama (2019). A former editor for Snow Lion Publications, she is a practicing psychotherapist and lives in New Orleans.